Opinions of Young Mature Minds

BRITTANY PHILLIPS

authorHOUSE®

AuthorHouse™
1663 Liberty Drive
Bloomington, IN 47403
www.authorhouse.com
Phone: 1-800-839-8640

First published by AuthorHouse   08/27/2011

ISBN: 978-1-4567-9645-7 (sc)
ISBN: 978-1-4567-9644-0 (ebk)

Library of Congress Control Number: 2011915817

Printed in the United States of America

Any people depicted in stock imagery provided by Thinkstock are models, and such images are being used for illustrative purposes only.
Certain stock imagery © Thinkstock.

This book is printed on acid-free paper.

Table of Contents

➢ Introduction 1

➢ God and Life 6

➢ Love 12

➢ Family 23

➢ Friends 30

➢ Respect 35

➢ Dreams 41

➢ Money 48

➢ Sex 53

➢ Government 62

➢ Miscellaneous 69

➢ Introduction of Part 2 92

➢ Overview 107

➢ Thanks 108

➢ About The Author 109

Introduction

Hi, my name is Brittany Phillips, starting this book at 15 years old, but who is to say when I will be through. I decided to write the book because I have a lot to say, some free time and I have started doing some serious thinking with my life.

I always wanted to help my mom, grandmas, aunt mary, and entire family because they always took care of me. So since I love to write, this book is an attempt to help older people understand the reasons us young people do some of the things we do, as well as help young people open their minds to maturity.

While these are just my opinions about life and what I wish could happen today, I've taken into consideration that all may not agree with everything I say. I am asking you to listen and read this with an open mind. If you don't agree with anything, I hope that you would consider why I believe the way I do. I really hope you enjoy the book, understand, and appreciate. Thank You.

<u>Princeton</u>

Princeton was a close friend of mines and I was the last person he saw when he died 3 blocks down from my house. It killed me because when you know you talked to someone last it shows you how short and crazy life is and it makes you think, why you? I couldn't even go to his funeral either so this poem was like closure for me. I loved him and he was a good friend,
RIP Princeton Watson.

Princeton

My friend Princeton

Man he's gone

We were gone be together forever

We tried so hard to hold on

That was my friend my best friend till the end

But who knew the end would come so fast

All because of a bike

And a stupid car crash

He was so young

Only 14

He had so much ahead

Man this boy had dreams

Some of his dreams consist of following in his father's footsteps

And some were the dreams of having his own family to help

I never thought we would have to say goodbye

At least not like this

We say goodbye

And then cry

But only if I had one wish

If I had one wish

Man I'd wish him next to me

I'd wish he was alive and standing here

And this was only a dream

Not even a dream

A horrible nightmare

He wanted to change his life

Dang I wish he were here

Why did he have to die

Why do people lie

Why can't we turn back the hands of time
Well I'm not glad he's gone
As I'm saying in this poem
But I'm glad he's in a better place
Now we just have to finish the race
You know what he'd say if he were here
"Man shut up"
I can hear it in my ear
Princeton I love you more than anything in the world
Glad you're in heaven watching us from above
Prize
Righteous
Intelligent
New to life
Christ child
Enormous heart
Tough
Outstanding
No one else like him
He's one in a million
Rest In Peace . . . .

God and Life

Life in the eyes of a young, Black, African-American female, it's crazy! It seems too much to handle, drama, boys, school, careers, test-test-test, family, church, but it's really not. Life is in the eye of the beholder, as in life is in God's hands. If you appreciate life and you are happy being able to wake up another day and breathe then you should thank God. Life doesn't always make you happy but when you think back it makes you glad. Life is full of choices you either make a right one or a wrong one; learn from your mistakes. Life isn't fair; who said it was? You have judgmental, rude, ungrateful, racist, and worst, just cruel hateful people. Don't expect everything to be fabulous . . . you'll be lying to yourself. But when it comes down to it life and God are all one; God created life for a reason and you live your life to a certain extent. God always has a plan for your life, and He knows what's going to happen before it does, so I believe everything happens for a reason; life is life you live it according to how you feel, what you <u>know</u> and <u>want</u>. All I can truly say is be careful what you ask for, you may get it. Make the right choices too because the wrong ones will be hard to pay for and you will never forget them..!!! My pastor says, "God works on His own time, He may not come when we want Him to, but He'll be there right on time". Everything happens for a reason, not always good and not always bad, but God will work it in your favor the way He wants it to.

I asked a friend what he would say if someone asked him what he thought about God and Life. Mannie said, "God is my support through good times and bad. Never put your trust in a man because he fails but God never changes. He should be your foundation when creating anything, because when storms come the base will not sway. As for life, it is what you make it. Like the Bible says," You should rejoice in the Spirit in good and bad times". So when people say life is horrible, I feel that if you want good in your life you should start with yourself and make the change. It is best to try and fail, than to have never tried at all. This way a person is given two chances; succeed or fail. We make the choice-God makes the change".

<u>Forgiveness</u>

You can't go to heaven holding a grudge. I had to learn just like the next person, and you will be so much better off if you just forgive. Grudges only hurt you in the end.

Forgiveness

When you try to forgive
It's like something pulling you back
Saying no don't do it
Even though it's right

The devil and angels on your shoulders
Arguing back and forth
But truly you know
It's really your choice

You have to decide to forgive or hold a grudge
If you forgive don't forget
If you grudge don't let it stick

Forgive with your soul
Don't grudge with your heart
Then you'll be able to see the light in the dark

Live, life, love
Love and live life
Forgive those who hurt you
So you can live right

I'm Dying Real Slowly

At times I felt like nobody cared about me life my, problems didn't matter but prayer changes. When you do what you know you should and just call on God it's not going to be automatic but He's going to be right there when you thought you were dead in it all.

I'm Dying Real Slowly

I'm dying real slowly

There's something tearing out my soul

I'm dying real slowly

My body is so cold

I feel so alone

Left out in a horrible world

Left like no one cares for me

I can only do wrong

I'm dying real, real slowly

I can feel my insides burning up

Can someone help me reach out and touch

Just one touch

I'm dying real slowly and in need that man

That man called my heavenly Father

To walk with me, talk with me, and lead me from trouble

I'm dying real slowly

And I do know what to but I'm afraid to do it

But don't be afraid too

If you feel like I do call on the Father

TRUST He'll be there for you

No matter the problem

Love

Boys, not knowing who to talk to, who to trust, who really cares about you physically and mentally, who wants you for you and not just want you to get in your pants. Even if it's just a friend that's a boy, is he really your friend or what does he want something from you? "Never give away something that you would want back (virginity for example)". The main saying of a young boy is; "If you love me you'll do it," trust me, if he loves you he wouldn't try to make you do something against your will, or put pressure on you. If he loves you, he should be willing to wait and not cheat in the process of waiting. As spoken by a friend, "Love is a bitch". It changes a person inside and out. Once love is there or you think it is, you do things you would never think of or imagine. I feel that love is a mark. Every time love shows up, it leaves a mark, whether happy or sad; it's a mark that will never go away, it's your reminder of what happened. I don't think anyone will ever be able to define love or know the true meaning or feeling unless it's like it was in the old days, how it was when things were done the right way. "Don't go to love, let it come to you". When you love someone there's no act to the end of things you'll give to that person even if they keep repeating themselves/mistakes over and over again, love makes you forgive and keep moving until it's officially abused. Love doesn't keep track of everything wrong you do, it isn't jealous, arrogant, or rude and when it's there and real it's tender and unconditional. Sometimes when you love someone you can find yourself in that person, in their life, in their eyes and if you can't maybe they're not for you. Love is a big risk and a huge chance, because with it you must be willing to put in work.

Another thing I was also informed about and agree with are the things a man and woman want out of a relationship regardless. A man wants respect plus etc, and woman wants love/affection. I honestly believe it because if you say we females are always complaining about quality time or whatever it might be, maybe because we don't feel that affection . . . WE WANT ATTENTION. Just like a man gets upset when he feels disrespected more than anything else, that's when he trips out the most, he wants his respect, no man wants to feel belittled or less of a man, especially by a woman. Also men and women love differently so that's why it has to be patience. Women love and love sincerely and care quicker that's why we get hurt more often. But when it comes to a man they love harder. They may not fall in love as quick as us, but when they do love, they love harder and may have a different way of showing it but when they do it's tougher. I'll take myself for example, I like attention, demand respect, and I like to be shown that I am appreciated. It doesn't always have to be the big things; the small ones are the ones that last a lifetime and are mostly remembered. When it comes to relationships I try to treat others as I want to be treated. I want to be heard and so I try to listen, I want to be respected so I respect them as well, if you don't give your partner what they want, how do you think they'll react when you want it, do you think they'll stick around? No matter what it is, if you won't do it, someone else will, and that's where a lot of people mess up and relationships crumble. Love comes with so many attachments, rules, and regulations; you might say that love has its own laws. Love can make you happy and become priceless or it can make you hurt and become costlier than life itself. People act like you can buy love at a store or like they can't love anyone; however, when you least expect it or don't think it's possible that is when it happens. I was once asked, "What do you do when you love someone but you have to leave for a while, do you trust them or leave them until you come back"? Do you trust them totally or do you take a break because it seems like the best thing to do? If you love someone and you don't want to hurt them, what do you do about it? If you trust yourself and them and you really love or care for that person shouldn't you stay with him/her? If you don't trust yourself/them and you still love or care for that person, do you decide whether you want to try or you want to save some hurt and let go until you are together again? I feel that if you don't have trust you don't have anything and that is one of the things you have to work out and come to an understanding about when you are in a relationship.

Quick question; do you let your friends determine your love for your partner? If your friend said you were stupid for having or not having sex with someone while you were "official" or not with your partner would you agree or disagree? Would you do things because your "friends" said something or have enough care, courtesy, and respect for yourself and your partner to do what is right? I wonder about it because that's also how a lot of relationships end up not working. Your friends may know what's best sometimes but they will never know that person like you know them, so they shouldn't have a real say in what goes on or the decisions you make. Don't let anyone even your family control your outcomes in your life, it's your life not theirs and you have to live with the choice not them!! Musiq Soulchild said it best, "Love so many things I've got to tell you but I'm afraid I don't know how because there's a possibility that you'll look at me differently". You say you love me, why would you look at me differently? If I told you the truth, the whole truth, and nothing but the truth about me, will you still look at me and smile regardless of what I say to you rather it's good or bad, if you love me? You should never settle if you're not happy. When you are in a relationship don't just try to make the other person happy when you aren't happy because eventually you are going to hurt that person worst now, than you would have from the start. Don't be a coward, (male or female) and just stop talking to that person, either be man or woman enough to say, "I'm sorry but it's not working out". Love is a fatal thing and nothing to toy with. Lives have been destroyed, terminated, and controlled all because of this little thing called love. "Love thru all the ups and downs the joys and hurt, love for better or worst I still will choose you first". Whether it is your mother or father, sister or brother, lover or partner, for better or worst, will you put that person before yourself or behind yourself? I remember reading this poem a long time ago, "If you love me like you told me please be careful with my heart, you can take it just don't break it or my world will fall apart" (author unknown).

<u>My First Kiss</u>

I think I wrote this poem when I was in 8th or 9th grade and it is something everyone relates to because everyone has or is going to have their first kiss. It's short, simple, and cute.

My First Kiss

Eww boy let me tell you bout my first kiss

My first real kiss that made me gliss

Gliss like the beautiful stars above

Like the twinkle in a babies eye

I was with my boo yea that's right

Chillin in the hall walkin by his side

We were walking down the hall then he gave me a hug

Then he kissed me on the cheek

Then we kissed with love

Ya'll always say we don't know what love is

But I'm telling you we got that young love jig

Made me want to fall flat off my feet

Man I can't wait till the next time

When we kiss again like the very first time

What's Love

Love is a two way street and it takes two people to make it work and anybody would agree with me. If you really love someone and you want the relationship or friendship to work even with family members no matter what somebody will be the bigger person and realize life is too short. Show you love them before it's too late, even if you are tired of it always being you first, either say something or continue with your routine, "Closed mouths don't get fed".

What's Love

I'm always saying
I love you and let's work it out
But why is it always me
Why am I at fault

It takes two to tango
Not just one to dance
Three's a crowd so what's left
Two holding hands

Love is strong
A passion that's a drug
Love shouldn't be played with
It's as dangerous as a gun

Love goes as deep as the blood
Running in your veins
Love shouldn't be toyed with
IT ISN'T A GAME

Love can get crazy so don't fall too easy
Be careful watch your back because it's not always breezy
Everyone thinks it but doesn't say it out loud
So I'm saying watch it because love can get wild

I Cheated

I cheated is a poem I wrote my freshman year in college and is pretty close to my heart. The song called "Me" by Tamia inspired it because you should put yourself and your feelings first before you adjust your life for a man, or a woman, you are your number one option especially when no one else cares.

I Cheated

I cheated and I'll admit

It felt so good

I needed the relief and less stress

The exhale of a deep breath the weight of the world crumbling down my shoulders

It made me feel better than you never did or ever could

Put a bumper sticker on your Bentley

Represent for my kid but disgrace your vehicle

Spoiled me like you should have

Held me when you didn't

Pushing into this thing called life Daddy's little girl

Went shopping with me and held my purse

Even if we were broke at least we spent time

Took me on the best dates ever out to eat, to the movies

I didn't know it could be this great

Kept me up beat and in shape

Didn't let me slip or slumber

I cheated but not with a man

With a woman who understood me better than I did myself

My mind reader, dream catcher

Knew my needs and wants and exactly how to fulfill them

The threesome was wonderful

The love we had streamed through my blood with another life itself

They knew how to change my frown to a smile

They'd die for me unlike you

Do anything to make me happy

Loved me for me regardless of what anybody said

They understood the person I was no assumptions necessary

I cheated

Started a new life
It was so hard to believe
But it wasn't with a man
Nor another woman
It was me, myself, and I
No companion needed

<u>Family</u>

I believe family is one of the most prized possessions in life, so you should always try to have a strong bond with your family. If you have only one person in your life, DON'T TAKE HIM/HER FOR GRANTED. As long as you know that there is one person in this world who loves you, don't worry about what anyone else thinks or says. Family always has your back, and will hold you up, and protect you. If your family doesn't then pray about it because families must have that strong hand that holds the family together so they can stick together. No matter how your family treats you, you should always remember next to God, family is the most important asset in life and if we continue to let satan take our men out of our households (a man is suppose to be the head of the household) then our children won't even know what a real home and family is. A family is like the world, different people, types, attitudes, cultures, but everyone needs love. Even when you feel like your world is falling apart or even when family does you the worst, they will always be there when you need them most, even if they aren't blood relatives, whoever you consider family as, that's your family.

Family is basically another word for togetherness, a collective strong loving bond, always with you, always there, and always supportive. For people who may not have a complete family, don't think that it has to be a mom and a dad and aunties and uncles, your family can be as simple as you and a relative or even a friend. My REAL friends are my family too. We may argue and fight but we never lose sight of what we have and of course we stay tight, that's what family does. Friends who are there for you when you are wrong or right are family, someone who helps you when you're down, that's family, someone who will surely be there in your time of need, is family. If you have that then YOU HAVE ALL YOU NEED. Families must be strong and stay together to survive, if you fight together, pray together, and never leave anyone behind, you are that one fist that will strike a mighty blow (as said in Soul Food).

Think before you do whatever it is you are thinking about doing because revenge is ripping our world and families apart, and sometimes we get revenge on the wrong people and for the wrong things. People always say just because they did it to me I'm going to get them back and I'm going to get them worst than they got me, but can you tell me what that will accomplish? It doesn't make you feel better unless you have no conscious, it doesn't make anyone happy it makes them sad, while providing another source for the news. Even worst I found out on the discovery channel that animals will fight, but NOT kill their opponent, but humans fight TO kill, so it makes me wonder who's the real animal?

If the people of this world could stick together as a family we wouldn't have any problems. We wouldn't have wars; we wouldn't have to kill just to get a dollar. Money isn't everything, but it sure is making this world go round and our families go down the drain. If everyone wasn't so greedy and treated the next person as they would their family then it wouldn't be a problem. Do you get tired of working so hard just to get by? Do rich people get tired of trying to stay rich? Building families builds character, and if this country, what we call our "Great America" was built with this concept in mind and kept this concept in mind then maybe this would truly be the GREATEST place in the world, especially to raise your family.

<u>You Feel Like No One Cares</u>

This speaks for itself. Once again in my life I felt this way but I got over it through expressing myself in a positive way that I know others can relate to. Rather it's your music or poetry or dance, etc find what makes you relax and clear your head because someone always cares.

<u>You Feel Like No One Cares</u>

Ya know sometimes I feel like no one cares
Like no one will care if I roll over, fall out, and die
Or no one cares how I feel about my life
Like no one cares about my life

I know you feel it too often sometimes
Like "Umm I wonder what would happen when I die"
How will my family feel, how would my lover feel
How would the lives of the ones I was close to go on

You feel like no one cares sometimes
I feel like no one cares sometimes
Do they care . . . let me ask them
"Do ya'll care about my life"

Just know when you think no one cares about you
God the Father our Father cares for you
He cares if you die for every tear your cry
He cares about your life your wrongs and your rights

You feel like no one cares but someone does
I found out by my mother about the guy above
Now you're finding out too, a little truth
God loves you and somebody like me cares for you too

<u>Father</u>

This poem was born during the summer of 2009 when I was in a summer program called Access at Prairie View A&M University. I was in a class that I felt like was made to make you think. I really liked the class because it was fun and helped me express myself. So we were suppose to write in this journal everyday and we got graded on what we wrote so I always wrote little things and poems and I started writing one about my father. I never realized until I was going through my book months later how my father being in and out of my life, but really not being their effected me. Not only males are affected by not having a father but females too, so this is it, how I feel.

Father

Sometimes I wonder am I cold-hearted
Am I wrong for not caring for my father
Maybe it did matter if you were there but you weren't so I taught myself not to care
Is that why I don't care much for boys who try to care for me
Is that why I push them away
Is that why I build up this electric fence to supposedly protect myself
Is that why I can be so violent
I'm gone hurt you before I let your hurt me because I'm not gone get got but do the getting
Deep inside I want that guy
The one who's suppose to be in my life
Left my brother, left my sister, and then left me a stray
Why did I have to be one of the same
Another statistic raised without a father
Fuck it I won't stand for that
It killed me not to see my father out there in the audience
Saw his father but not mines
It's like a hole in my heart that only he can fill
Every time he's missing at an important event in my life
Even though I hate to admit it, it takes another chunk out of my life
Takes away the celebration
Makes 18 years not matter
Makes 18 years dissolve
Makes me feel as though my life didn't matter
Like I didn't matter to him at all
What did I do to deserve this
You knew what you were getting into
You knew 1 + 1 = 3

You and my mom made me so what happened
I'm just asking for an answer
NOT AN EXCUSE
But you don't know how to do that
So I gave up I don't care now at all

Friends

Be careful who you trust or call your friend because the one you trust the most maybe the one to hurt you the MOST. Tyler Perry states, "Some people are in your life for a season and some are here to stay, some people are roots, branches, or leaves in your life", and its best for you to know which people are which. Are they the leaves that come and then flow away in the wind, the branches that hang for a while but eventually break away, or the roots in your life that are basically here to stay? Who are your friends in your life? Whether you believe it or not, you will only have one true friend, some people are lucky to have more than one real friend like myself, but it's not promised to have many people that care. I guarantee you'll have one person who cares for you and you can call a friend rather you know it or not, think about it. It's not much you can say, but actions speak louder than words. Someone who treats you well explains with actions what you are to them; love is an action word as well as friendship. Know who your friends are, be open minded and focused on what you do, say, and how you act (treat people) and vice versa. Always remember:

*If your real friend loves you they can say it

*If your real friend cares they won't let anyone hurt you

*If your friend is real he/she won't hurt you and will be there for you when you are hurt

To find your real friend you should know that you can trust them. Its like a relationship, trust is the key. Anybody can do bad all by themselves, a real friend won't bring you down, but help build you up. You should be able to depend on them but also be dependable yourself, because a friendship is 50/50 and works both ways. A friend is that person that is there for you when you need them or not and you should always determine your friends by who they really are and not what they do for you or have.

Askjeeves.com defines the word friends as: a person whom one knows, likes, and trust-an acquaintance. But a friend is also someone you can call sister or brother, mother or father, someone to literally ride or die with you. It's funny that I say this because I once received a chain letter by text that related to this. It stated: "A simple friend, when visiting acts like a guest but a real friend opens your refrigerator and helps himself. A simple friend doesn't know your parents first names but a real friend has their phone numbers in their address book. A simple friend brings a bottle of wine to your party but a real friend comes early to help you cook and stays late to help you clean. A simple friend hates it when you call after they've gone to bed. A real friend asks what took so long to call. A simple friend seeks to talk with you about your problems, but a real friend seeks to help you with your problem. A simple friend wonders about your romantic history, but a real friend can blackmail you with it. A simple friend thinks the friendship is over when you have an argument. A real friend calls you after you had the fight. A simple friend expects you to always be there for them, a real friend expects to always be there for you. A simple friend bails you out of jail when you get in trouble but a real friend is sitting next to you saying DAMN WE MESSED UP"! It's not much more you can say about friends, because all you'll be doing is repeating yourself over and over again. You know your friends and you know your foes, you know who's real and who needs to walk out your door. But do remember don't be blinded by lies and foolish material things because a true friend is something you get once in a lifetime. Also remember if someone says they're your friend they will respect you whole heartily and not judge you because you do your own thing. They will respect you, your parents, and their elders; they will respect your house and your things, THEY WILL RESPECT YOU!

What a friend isn't:

*a person who lies for no reason claiming to protect your feelings

*people who will do you wrong and think nothing of it as if they were the victim
*a person who will abandon you when you need them most
*a person who says they're your friend but doesn't show it/has a hell of a way showing it

What a friend is:
*a person who will tell you the truth regardless because they don't want to see you in pain
*a person you can trust to know they won't seriously blackmail you with anything
*a person you can chill with even if they get on your nerves, but still not be able to live without them
*a person who will save you in life or death situations risking their own
Do you know who your friends are?? Are you a real friend??

<u>JJ</u>

This poem was written to a dear friend of mine I meet in the summer access program of 2009. She shared her story with me and it was touching, to see someone be so strong and come thru what she did, it inspired me and gave me a new respect for her and the things I've been thru.

JJ

When you're able to come from the ground up you are stronger
When you can make it through so much that's when you're stronger
When you can make the best out of a situation that's when you're stronger
When you can speak up on your past that's when you're stronger
When you can forget the bad and continue on that's when you're growing
When you take responsibility for something that's not your fault you're growing
When you are that mom or that dad or whoever you weren't from the beginning you're growing
Excuses are like assholes everybody has one
But if you choose not to use it you are better than what people say you are
If you choose not to take the easy way out you are better than what people say you are
When you prove them wrong you are better than what they say you are
When you use your pain in a positive way instead of a negative way you are better than what they say you are
You are strong, you are bold, you are what most people want to be
You keep believing in God and keep the faith cause' you see how you were and how far you came to be.
(Dedicated to J.J.)

Respect

R-E-S-P-E-C-T Aretha Franklin says it best, "find out what it means to me". Respect is one of the most important aspects in the world. Everyone should have respect for themselves and for everyone else too. It can get you killed, hired, fired, feared, cared for, and so much more. As females you should respect yourself as number one top priority, because it you don't who will? As males you should do the same but also respect females, most people don't realize that you don't have a say so of how you are raised until you are old enough to know better and some females don't know better and if you disrespect them some people just get used to it, but that doesn't mean its right! This subject is one of the most talked about and most honored subjects in the world. It is something that no matter whether you notice it or not it will be the topic floating in the air. Respect is defined as, to feel or show esteem; reframe from violating; to treat with consideration. You respect people, things, animals, rules, and just about whatever else you can think of, or at least you are suppose to. Respect, like money is a major issue to life. When you show and give respect to others in whatever you do, it determines how high you get, and what you get in life. It reminds me of a little phrase I learned called "burning your bridges"—If you show someone that you can't be trusted they'll never ask you again for whatever it was because you've basically burned your bridge. Your bridge was trust and you lost that trust when you didn't stick to your word. I used that to say, you can burn your bridge with <u>lies</u> and <u>deceit</u> or you can build your bridge with <u>respect</u> and <u>truth</u> because when you disrespect someone, then they won't give you the respect you want. When you disrespect people it shows them your true colors and they won't ever let you do it again, you have burned your bridge and lost your respect, but was it worth it? If you respect someone you can build a sturdy bridge, but disrespect will always burn down to the ground. You should always respect people regardless of age, gender, body type, or cultural background. All people were born with it and deserve to have it just as much as the next person. Ignoring age, gender, or race you never know what they can offer or help you with, (you never know who you are talking to).

Do you believe that you should respect your elders and all people period? If not, why? Why do you think that you deserve respect but you don't have to give it to anyone else, why do you think that you are any more deserving? Is it the fact that, that's simply the way you were taught, or just you simply don't care? Respect starts from the people living on the streets to the rich people in the suburbs. Just like the rich look down on us we look down on the next group and who gave us the right to say we are better, we definitely know nothing about them. Who gave us the right to look down our nose at someone else like we are better than they are, we don't like it, so, do you think they do? NO! SHOW RESPECT! I can't stress why respect is such a big factor in this world, but some people just don't realize how much it matters to give and you shall receive, give people the same thing you'd want someone to give back to you. Like Tyler Perry's movie, <u>The Family That Preys</u>, states, "everybody's got a story to tell, you might be entertaining an angel", or being disrespectful to one!!

<u>Question</u>

This poem was just thought about because I really do wonder how some people just decided to treat people how they want to treat them instead of the right way.

Question

How far does it stretch
How far does it go
Where do you determine the length it flows
Does it stop at the poor or stop at the rich
The less fortunate
Or the fortunate of wit

It's rather noble in its own manner
Recognized and honored
For what it is, it's been, it is today
For who gets it, who doesn't, who wishes, who prays
It's more than it seems
What is appears to be

How far does it stretch
How far does it go
Who receives it from the starting post
Respect

<u>Really</u>

I was thinking about how come when people's attitudes change towards someone all of a sudden what they mean to you change. Now they have a new name . . . really??

Really

How come she's a bitch or a hoe when you're mad at her but when you're not she's your angel

But ladies how come he's a low down dog when you're mad but the best man ever when you're not

Make up your mind

Choose your thoughts

What gives you, us, whoever the right to label someone

To treat someone wrong just because you're mad

I don't care if you're mad at whatever you control your thoughts

Cause from the abundance of the heart the mouth speaks

And it may not be a lot to you

But it falls in deep with me

Dreams

I always get the same advice when it comes to dreams. I am constantly being told, "You can do it if you believe, keep your head up and don't give in, you can do it no matter what anyone says". They never tell you how hard it is and the roads you have to choose with your dreams. The truth is always sugar coated. They tell you the sky is the limit, but why does it take so long when you're moving closer and closer every day, or so you thought? They make it seem like since the sky is the limit you can do whatever you want, but can you? You have to put up with stupid, ignorant, and greedy people who try to stop you, the real limit isn't the SKY but somewhere in between striving toward your dream and almost there. Your dreams can be reached but you have to be ready for whatever God gives you or has planned. Sometimes you even want to give up because things may not go your way and I totally understand, but sometimes you just have to say f . . . the world. Whenever you think of giving up or you want to stop trying just say f . . . the world. Say to yourself that you can do anything and do it. You know that's where we often mess up because we just say it, but we don't take action. I attended a National Conference for "The Urban League" in the year of 2008 where the theme was "Got Dream? See It, Own It, Do It". That's what we should do, if you have a dream see your dream, own your dream, and accomplish that dream.

Your dreams shouldn't be determined by what other people have or by what is shown on T.V. It should be measured by what you really want, like those dreams you had when you were a child and when you thought of what you wanted to be when you grew up. Take those into consideration; it wasn't by accident that that's what you wanted. The fake dream is in a way how Nas states, "Street dreams are made of these 'N' push Beemer's and 300 E's, a drug dealer's destiny is reaching a key, everyone's looking for something, shorties on their knees for 'N' with big G's who am I to disagree, everybody's looking for something". Do you really want your dream to be you looking for some dude who can take care of you financially or better yet material wise? Does he actually care about you or just loves the THINGS you do for him?? You can't be serious if you think he does because everything comes with a price, rather you know it or not. That wasn't your childhood dream. Do you really want the lifestyle of being a groupie, gold digger, or somebody's baby mama or even daddy? Everybody's looking for something but what are you looking for? Are you looking for the right thing or the right ring?? The ring that will lead to a life of loneliness if it isn't real. Why don't we help each other? We are a group of individuals who used to stick together thru thick thin, rain, sleet, hail, or snow and now it's like "whatever". Why won't we help that fallen brother or sister in time of need to reach their dream? Maybe it's just too many crabs in the barrel trying to bring each other down instead of pushing each other to the top. Is this not one of our dreams as a people, was this not Martin Luther King Jr's dream for us to be one united together? Not just blacks, but all races and cultures should work together, but we fail to help the next person up. Why is this not our dream, instead of being a video vixen or super skinny model, or having the most money, what's wrong with our priorities and choices in life? What was the big thing that made us change and not see the true and real meaning of life anymore? Better yet to say, why haven't we found and captured the true meaning of life? I'm guessing that just wasn't one of our dreams. We just left behind a firefighter, or policeman, or doctor, or lawyer, not for the money but to make our world a great place to live in. I believe that not just children, but the world is the future and in the words of Michael Jackson, "we need to start with the man in the mirror" to bring dreams back. Don't dream of being a follower or an outcast, but dream to be different and to be true (true to yourself first but everyone else as well). Dream to dream!

Now that Barack Obama is the President of the United States of America it is like all dreams can come true, no matter what. As many times as I've heard it I believe it and agree, "When a child says he/she wants to be president that it's not a myth but a dream reality waiting to happen". Obama is the new addition, and the best thing that happened to America and the best dream revealed to a child. "Dreams are real all you have to do is just believe" (Ashanti). When you have the determination, the spirit, the drive to do what you have to do to get what you want, nothing can stop you. Alicia Keys says, "We could fight like Ike and Tina, or give back like Bill and Camille, be rich like Oprah and Steadman, or instead struggle like Flow and James Evans . . . . Cause he ain't no different from you and she ain't no different from me, we have to live out our dreams like the people on TV, we gotta stay tuned cause there is more to see, through the technical difficulties, we might have to take a break but ya'll know we'll be back next week..". We could bury our dreams like they never existed to us or live them like the people we admire, cause we are no different, we just take different paths.

Martin Luther King Jr. said, "I have a dream", and Barack Obama said, "Yes We Can" and we did. This was all a dream, now seeing inter-racial couples, and different races and genders working together side by side, and November 4, 2008, a black man became president which people only saw as a dream now a reality, we did it! The day a black man became the 44th president of the United States of America was the end of a long journey from the 13th amendment that freed slaves, to the 26th amendment that gave 18 year olds the right to vote. God has it all planned out, "those which were last will one day be first", do you believe it is coming or even here? Do you think MLK's dream is still deferred or reincarnated? Listen to the words of a nursery rhyme (that was brought to my attention), "Row, row, row your boat gently down the stream, merrily, merrily, merrily, merrily life is but a DREAM! Live yours!!

<u>Don't</u>

This is about not letting anyone change your mind about anything. If you want to do something then just do it, don't stop until you get it because the only true person that can stop you is you. Look at me, I wrote a book and people told me I couldn't do it but I proved them wrong, and it feels so good!

Don't

Don't ever let it be deferred or taken from you

Don't ever let it die because you don't know where it would take you

Don't let it run away or vanish in your mind

Be lost and never again found

Don't let it be buried or hidden under a tomb stone

Be cremated or burned to the ground

Don't let it get kidnapped and not returned

Be devoured and destroyed

Don't let it be run over by a car

Be buried in a fire

Don't let it commit suicide or be apart of manslaughter

Be murdered or hung from trees in a forest

Don't let it be stolen in a robbery

Be shot in a drive by

Protect it, love it, live it, and lift it high

Your dreams are your dreams and don't have to die . . .

Dream Of

Dream of is saying that instead of looking at life in a negative view, look at all the positive or imagine it as positive and it'll feel better. Look at the glass half full instead of half empty (note: always remind yourself that it's somebody somewhere worst off than you are and you accomplishing your dream may help them).

Dream Of

Dream of beauty
Dream of life
Dream of love
And sweet viewing sites

Dream of joy
Dream of peace
Dream of birth
How sweet it can be

Dream of Christmas
Dream of toys
Dream of goodness
And what children adore

Dream of music
Dream of poems
Dream of books
And the arts of the world

Dream of ballads
Dream of melodies
Dream of change
We sincerely need

Dream of people
And what we should be
Of gone away pains, mirrors of no shame
Magic in the air, and moons of care

Money

Do you let money run your life? You think, "Oh I got this money, I'm bout to buy this and that, get this tight ride, and halla at these hoes", NO!! That's stupid and you are giving the people who are making money off of you, more power and providing what they thought you would; a better life for them and false beliefs for you. The reason they test us so much in schools is not to find out what we learned, but how many prisons they have to build. They don't care about providing you a good education, that's why you have to TAKE IT. Instead of playing in class listen, even if you don't want to PAY ATTENTION. I know sometimes you just want to have fun because even I clowned but I knew when I could clown and when it was time to take care of business. Be top in your class and getting scholarships, have someone else pay for your school so your parent(s) don't have to, and get the ones with the money to spend it on your education, that you once couldn't have received years ago but have the chance to today.

Have you ever thought about how money is the root of all evil? You shouldn't let money control you or make you who you are. They print money everyday and God forgive me but only fools fight for it and go through what they do for nothing. They kill themselves and hurt each other over paper that other people could care less about; because once you are gone they have your money in the end anyways. Once you're dead and lying in a coffin somewhere they can care less about whom you are, what you are, or rather who you were. To them that's just one less 'N' on the streets. Don't get me wrong when I say 'N' because it's not just black people but its whites/Caucasians, Indonesians, Asians, Hispanics, Mexicans, whatever and whoever. The word is technically defined as a stupid or ignorant person and NOT ONE OF COLOR!

Tommy Ford said and I agree that, (a little rephrased for understanding) "You are born with 100% potential and it's up to you if you use it in your lifetime. In realization the graveyard is the richest place on earth because that's where people are buried with the 100% potential they were born with because they chose not to use it or only used some of it". When you let money rule you in everything you do you don't use your full potential, you use money to get everything instead of your hard work.

I remember being at Kashmere Senior High School's 2008 Athletics Banquet and our keynote speaker said something that I will always remember, "It wasn't always my fault but it was my problem". The life he had wasn't his fault but it was his problem, and he lived thru it and became a better person and a accomplished man. It's not fair that it is your problem when it's not your fault. It isn't fair and we say life isn't fair, but we also say life is what we make it. So when we say life is what we make it, are we saying that we made life unfair and not the things God allowed to happen was created unfair? Are we saying that it's not fair that we let money rule our lives but it's our problem. Instead of being fixated on making money any way possible, we should be concentrating on making a good life with what we have and/or earned. We don't want to make money our main focus because that's how people destroy their lives. Forgetting the ones they care for, for the things that don't care for them. Life is what we make it and if we want a happy life we should make it free of stress, pain, anguish, and money issues (keep faith in God). If we the people or rather, we the consumers have less of a demand then prices going up will come down. Try to make a change in your life like try to recycle, save paper, recycle cans, any aluminum, and quit smoking would save us and save a lot of money and time wasted (time is money and money is time). It is so much that we could do to better our world and overall our lives. Diddy said it, "Mo money mo problems"!!

Who's Fault

This poem was thought of when I realized a lot of things we have to deal with in life may not have been our fault but ended up as our problem and we had to learn how to fix it. A lot of that will happen to us but the objective is not to complain but to fix it and get something from it, learn from it and you can help someone else out if the same thing may happen to them.

Who's Fault

Is it that child's fault for being the way he or she is
Is it that girls fault for the way that she's built
Is it that boys fault for thinking like the average boy
Is it that mothers fault for not always being able to bring joy
Is it that fathers fault for being taken away from his home
Is it anyone's fault for all the wrong that's done
It's a question that floats in the air daily never being answered but I do have a comment
I was once told that it's not my fault but it's my problem says the speaker
It wasn't his fault for the circumstances he grew up in but it became his problem
It's not that child's fault for not knowing better but it's that child's problem
It's not that girls fault for the way she's built but it is her problem
It's not that boy's fault that he thinks likes that but it's that boy's problem
It's not that mothers fault she's not perfect but it's that mothers problem
It's not that father's fault he left but it's that father's problem
It's not necessarily anyone's fault for wrong but its everyone's problem
We never take responsibility for our actions and were always looking for someone to blame
We may be the most innocent, humble, and sweetest people that never do wrong or not intentionally
But whatever was done becomes our problem so we have to acknowledge that fact and fix that problem
Stop blaming someone else and fix our problems
Stop killing ourselves and fix our problems
Stop hating each other and fix our problems

Start loving ourselves and fix our problems

Cause it may not be our fault but it's totally our problem and that's not going to change

Sex

To my girls first and foremost, we always hear people telling us, "YOUR VIRGINITY IS YOUR MOST SACRED POSSESION", believe it! You should never give away something you might want back, because once it's gone it's gone forever and you will NEVER get it back. It's true and that should say enough but in plain English just don't have sex if you're not ready, even when you think you are. You should never do anything for anyone else to make them happy, if you're not. What are they doing for you?

To my brothers, to my boys, SLOW DOWN. You shouldn't try to make a female do something she doesn't want to do, or isn't ready for even if she says she is. Sex is a very complicated thing. It makes a situation more complex to deal with mostly if you get addicted or get attached. Sex is like love, its pain, hurt, and joy all in one; you don't know what's going to happen it just does. When you get ready to give your virginity away and keep giving your body away before you are married you should think. Think ahead to the future, every time you have sex with someone else you are taking away from your husband/wife over, and over, and over again. If you can save it for the love of your life, when you're sure it's the love of your life, and not just a lesson or love in your life, do just that. Sex shouldn't be used for a frustration release or a headache pill or something just to make you feel good. Think about it when you have sex you are creating something special and wonderful, sometimes creating life. You don't want that to be an accident or a mistake. Like IMX sings, "It's nothing like the first time" or "You'll never forget your first time". Some people even wish they could go back to their first time to make it more special than it was, but it's already passed so they have to accept the choice they made (ask someone). Make sure your first time is with that special boy or girl!! Sex is a bond and should become a lifetime commitment; something you will share for the rest of your life with that one special person.

With AIDS and HIV and other things out there who would want to just give it away to anyone? Don't think just because someone has money or their outer appearance is up to par (A1) that they can't get or have anything. The cover of the book can be misleading. Another thing (as if I haven't heard it enough personally) I'm tired of people saying how the Black and Hispanic communities are at the highest risk. I'd rather hear positive speculations instead of negative ones. I'm tired of my race being the head statistic of the bad things and never the good ones. Someone had a dream for us, but we didn't seem to buy into that dream, did we? Even now when we watch BET they are keeping us abreast of the news by telling how our HIV status is rising daily because people won't get tested or won't get their results. Sadly to say, it's more 12-21 year olds getting tested to find out their status when there shouldn't be any at all. Instead of waiting till we are married or even the right one, we are just waiting until he says, "I love you"(rather it's real or not) or until the "Mr. right now" comes along. I received a chain letter from a friend that said "A girl will fake a orgasm for a relationship and a boy will fake a relationship for a orgasm". Doesn't that bother you how true that is and how embarrassing that is?

I was once told and I agree that between the ages of 15-25 a boy doesn't want anything but to get all of his "wild time" out of the way and have a good looking female on his arm, if he wants and when he wants. When he is 25-35 he's about ready to settle down trying to get his self together, but between the ages of 35-45 he's wiser and trying to let other males know about what they are doing at 15-25. It seems that no one is listening, because it's too many fatherless homes so people aren't willing to listen to no one else. I have my own little belief though, I believe that a boy/man doesn't stay around long enough to have a relationship and that's why I wouldn't have sex with every person I talk to; people make mistakes but, your mistakes don't matter if you don't learn from them (they say they're too young to be a boyfriend but not too young to have sex or have a baby). I realize that most relationships at young ages only last 3-6 months on average and that's the getting to know you stage, not having sex stage. Also in that time frame if you are having sexual relations than after that 3-6 months if either one <u>gets tired of it</u>, or <u>let's something get to them</u> then they break-up, it makes you wonder, what was there to keep them other than sex?

The Epitome of A Black Woman

I was at a spring break camp when I wrote this and our sponsor wanted each person to perform something that night at our talent show. So two girls and myself got together and performed, "The Epitome of A Black Woman" and it was such a success that we got the chance to perform it for Cicely Tyson herself, what an experience!

The Epitome of A Black Woman

Would you want to wake up every morning knowing that it's something inside you that just won't go away

Making you weaker and weaker no matter how hard you pray

The torcher and hurt haunts you everyday sticking to what statistics say

Always talking down on the black race

What is this why did I get this is this punishment for things that I've done

Maybe I shouldn't have done what I done when I did what I did how I did what I did when I did which was very stupid

Tell me do you get it

I am the epitome of a black woman

Look into my eyes and see what has been and what is yet to come.

<u>Never Gonna Get It</u>

I kind of got the idea from a song because it's a good song for girls to play for boys , but seriously it is something that girls shouldn't be afraid to say because what we have, no one should be able to take from us or let it be given away freely.

Never Gonna Get It

Never gonna get it
Is what I keep telling these boys
Never gonna get it
And I ain't no toy
Not something you can just use then pass on
I'm a human being
So you should treat me like one
Ya'll came from a woman get ya'll name from a woman
Everything from a woman and ya'll still do us wrong
Why do ya'll not care for us
Why do ya'll want to burry us
If it weren't for woman
Nobody would be born
If it wasn't for us
We would have all gone wrong

How Do You

How do you was written when I had my boyfriend in college and in reality he was the best boyfriend I had really had in a while so I was thinking maybe it's too good to be true but maybe it's not . . . . (it was; go with your gut feeling sometimes it usually knows what it is talking about).

How Do You

How do you choose to choose when the choices you've made before
have been just as blind as the one now
You follow your heart and get screwed
Follow your mind and get screwed
Follow what other people suggest and yet still get screwed
So I ask
How do you make a choice you never made before
How do you know the good or bad outcome if you haven't been there
before
How do you choose not to get hurt, lied to, or screwed over
Every time you are blind folded and reach your hand into the bag hoping
to get a good marble yet it's always a chance you won't
So
How do you handle it over and over again
Getting dropped just to pick yourself up again usually without help
How do you get used to holding yourself at night
How do you get used to getting lied to and deceived
How do you except failure and pain

Government

You know what needs to happen with the communities? We need to unite and stay united! Have you ever wondered how other races such as Caucasians, Asians, and etc., run their communities and ours too, it's because they stick together as one. The black community is weaker now than it was in the older days. People stuck together through trials and tribulations, they didn't let each other down, their word was their bond, and it was strong. Today its not like that. We kill our own people, do our own people wrong, we hurt our own woman, and treat one another worst than trash! THAT'S NOT UNITY AND THAT'S NOT ONE. "Every finger on your hand separated can't do damage but all those fingers balled up together can strike a mighty blow", (Soul Food). That is what we need to take back our government, "FOR THE PEOPLE, BY THE PEOPLE!" Tupac said, "We ain't ready to see a black president" and my question to you is in the year 2008 and the years that have come, with a black man and a white woman running for the presidency are we ready to see that? It's not the first time to my knowledge that a black man has run for president, but in this election it started with black man and a white woman, then a black man verses a white man, then the black candidate won, were we ready? Can we handle it or will some ignorant person who's still stuck in the "1600's" try to take away what could be the best thing to happen to America? Is America ready and willing for change? I can say personally that I, a Young Black, African American woman in today's society, I'm ready for change. Im ready for things to get better and stop getting worst and continuing with republicans in office that won't happen. I feel that they only care for themselves and that is part of the reason that the world is going to burn in a fiery hell because of the selfish and greedy acts of the people who don't care that they are sinning. Republicans don't care about anyone but themselves so why should we continue to let them stay in office when our voices and votes could change that ALL!!!! Its time for change and I'm up for it.

We shouldn't be separated by culture but joined by our differences. If our government won't do it then who will? If we don't take a stand and tell them what we want then we can't expect to get what we want-if we really want it. It's the governments' job to protect the people, but are they doing that? When they don't even care to give us affordable well fair or immigration reform, that shows me that the government doesn't care rather we live or die (republicans). We are all the same, many personalities, colors, and backgrounds but we are all "suppose" to be equal, living, breathing, human beings with the same needs and wants. Politics is a hard subject to talk about, it upsets me just thinking about the different points of views people have. The ones that upset me the most are the wealthier people who like I previously stated, only care about themselves and their own kind. They are only concerned with spending money to better their communities and areas, but nothing for us! Not being raciest but I believe that most Caucasians haven't worked 90% of their lives compared to some other races who have worked 99% of their lives almost including the day they were born, and the wealthy/ republicans have the nerve to say what we should and shouldn't have when they have no idea what it is like to live in this world with this life! The "minorities" get the leftovers and handouts while others get the best. If the government/republicans cared (like Obama DOES) they would help us out and quit with all the small talk and broken promises. Tell me what has our GOVERNMENT done about it? I'm tired of seeing homeless people mostly blacks on the streets; don't get me wrong we must give some of the blame to the people themselves, but until we sit and talk with them we can't blame it all on them because it may not be their fault. It isn't always their fault but unfortunately their problem, but why wasn't the government (before Obama) there when they needed a hand just that one time, especially for retired soldiers, elderly, and mentally handicap *citizens?* That's why I'm going to be one to make a change and a difference in life. I am going to make an honest change to my community, where I grew up and areas worst than mines, not being like the government, who you can't always depend on especially as a "minority".

Saying that brings me to my next thought, with all these "better and new" schools being built for "us" are they really for us? Why are these schools being built so far that a bus won't even come to pick our children up? How do they expect them to get a better education at a school they have no transportation to? Will the schools provide the services that the children need? Will we have teachers not care to teach because they assume the children don't care? Either do your work or fail becomes the teachers' attitudes or, as long as they are still getting their check . . . ?? Why put children in a situation where education is suppose to be taught but no one is doing their job, they have nothing to read, and no way of getting the education they desire. Where in the H-E—double hockey stick is our "GOVERNMENT"?

Part of The Message Part 4

Who else is tired of the war besides me? I'm tired of worrying about my loved ones overseas and scarred that one day my mom might have to go. I wish it would have never got this far and someone did something other than allow it. Everyday somebody is dying but is it truly for our country?

The Message Part 4

What do you think about this thing called war
It's so crucial, it's wrong so sad and well dumb
These people out here every day risking their lives
The fighting the fighting the torcher the cries
A soldier dies
We cry
But then they send out more
To continue the fight
What are we there for
What do we stand for
Can you tell me
The message part 4 . . . .

The Message Part 5

This poem is close to my heart because while it's one of my older poems I'm tired of seeing people die behind nonsense and then come black history time, we see how much our people have accomplished, and the only thing we accomplish now is going in and staying out of jail or the grave. What happened now from back in the days?

The Message Part 5

U-N-I-T-Y we forgot what that means

F-R-E-E-D-O-M we never really seen

L-O-V-E we say we know what that is

But G-O-D is what it really is

We forgot how to unite like the black panthers back in the days

We stopped being strong together and went our separate ways

We hurt our own people and truly didn't care

And still do now but act like we don't see it there

We become blind when people tell us what we don't want to know

But we crunk when our "friends" say "aye my nigga come on"

We don't unite now in the times young

So what our people fought for we may never see come

The way we act today we'll never see true freedom

Acting so dumb in society always having a gun

Just screams out "BEAT HIM"

You think that's cool and you think that's fly

NO, it's really cool to fight for real things and survive

Ya'll don't want freedom ya'll just want to get by

But you know what I think when it rains outside

That's not the time, but those are God's tears when He's crying

It makes me sad to see how far the world has fallen

So you just tell me what is that pouring

<u>Miscellaneous</u>

SOME OF MY OLDER POEMS FROM EIGHT GRADE

-Black Race

The black race

Sometimes a disgrace

The black on black crime

Living in this time

They trying to make us disappear

Listen up listen here

We always fighting

We need to be untied

Stand tall stand strong

Not weak and wrong

Don't give them what they want

Just make them front

-Do You

Do you want to be surrounded

With haters

And clown head

With loser

And smoochers

With people wishing

They could change their life

Wishing to change their wrong to right

Growing to a different height

Every night

Saying mama help me with this fight

Last breathe to breath

HELP ME PLEASE

-Drugs

To be drug free

It's the best way to be

It's the hottest in the spot

Drugs went from hot to not

From dark days to light days

From wrong ways

To good days

The best way to be

Is to be drug free

Just Like Me

-It Kills

It kills to see the struggle

Of my little bitty brother

My little sista crying

All my homies dying

Killing and stealing

Is what they all do

It kills to see you in the struggle you go through

It kills to steal

Good to rebuild

Bad to cry

Good to live

Poor people dying

Rich people trying to kill the different race-s

IT KILLS IT KILLS!!!!!!!!

SOME OF MY NEWER POEMS FROM 2000-UP

(These poems were inspired by many situations that I came across in the past couple of years. I hope that they make you second guess the outlook that you want people to see when they look at you or talk about you.)

<u>Destroyed</u>

I hate when good people make dumb decisions and stuff aka shit
happens that could have been prevented or helped
When people do stupid stuff and the punisher damages instead of
giving second chances
I especially hate when it's your own race black, white, or whatever and
you kill your own next generation but hate when someone else does it
I hate when you could understand that it was just one of those dumb
choices people make in life but you don't care at the moment
I hate when they can look at you and still destroy your future
I hate when they can look you in your face and still destroy your future
I HATE WHEN THEY CAN LOOK YOU IN YOUR FACE AND STILL
DESTROY YOUR FUTURE . . .

They Say

They say you never get what you ask for or just be

careful what you ask for

They say life isn't fair and nothing in life is free

Put your wants in one hand and piss in the other and see which one

fills up first

The sky is the limit

Life is what you make it

Love and live life

Solid as a rock

Live life to the fullest

Live your life as if it's your last day

They say we are all equal

You determine your future

If you don't know your past you can't make your present

Be the best you can be

Be a good role model cause someone's always watching

It's not what you know it's who you know

They say they say but who are they?

<u>Why</u>

Why do you tear down what you can build up
Why do you destroy what you can create
Why do you smash what you can mold
Why do you break what you can make

I ask myself these questions whenever I see things that just don't make
sense to me
Men always complain about how young men need some guidance and
someone to look up to
But if no one does it what do they have to look forward to
What are they to do when it's nothing but society, the environment, the
t.v., the video games, and the radio, the media, the internet, that are
raising our youth instead of our men

It pisses me off when people put off what they could be doing for
someone else to do
That's like letting the blind lead
Instead of the person with 20/20 vision
I ask why do you walk pass the piece of trash instead of pick it up

Why do you kill the child instead of let it live
Why do you let the animals stray instead of guide them
Why do you let the young black men go instead of revive them

Do We

Do we have to act immature

We are put in adult situations but act childish

We are treated like adults

But act as children

Do we have to be immature

We are talked to like we have sense

But we talk back like we have none

We are acknowledged with knowledge

But reply with none

Do we have to be ignorant

Dumb founded or unknowing to the fact of maturity

Unknowing to the idealism of wisdom

Do we have to be ignorant

Act without thinking

Pissed at the consequences you end up facing

<u>Perfect</u>

I am perfect because I have flaws

I am perfect because I'm not counterfeit

I am perfect because I'm not the skinny girls in the magazines

I am not the girl on t.v.

I'm unique

I am my own shape, form, and fashion

I am perfect because I have my human ways of course

I get angry and want to get even just like you

I don't wake up cute

I have my bloated days

I'm not you

I'm not him, I'm not her, I'm not trying to be you, her, or it

I'm not flawless, I'm not bruise less, I'm not a follower

I am perfect because I am ME!

ME

Why do you blame me for my looks, is it my fault I'm this way

I'm not perfect I was just taught how to make my looks sway

You get mad at me because I'm unique because I choose to be cool
with everybody

Cause for ya'll sake you should be happy I'm this way because you'd
hate to see the other me

You blame me for others actions, but you can't stop people from doing
what they want

Can anybody stop you from your free will

No

Exactly they can't

So I ask again why blame me

Just because I'm not insecure and was taught to have confidence

If I listened to what people say I wouldn't be where I am today

You're mad at me just because I'm always smiling

If I was always frowning you'd complain about that too

Damn what do you want from me

How bout you jump into my shoes

Be me for one day,

Be cordial to everybody so they'll be no drama

Try to keep giving respect cause if you lose yours, you might lose it

Try to keep your head up through the day and not let anything get you down

And try to just chill regardless to how people pressure you to stay around

Try to stay cute so your confidence will stay boosted

Try to stay happy so you won't lose it

Try to be the nice old fashioned young lady or man you were raised to be

Even though with people these days those morals are thrown out freely

Since they don't know why you act the way you do

People just judge you

People judge you constantly and won't leave you alone

But you keep your feelings to yourself and don't let anyone know

So again why do you blame me for not being you

I'm not you, I'm me, simply me so simply be you

(This poem basically means that you don't know why people do the things they do, you don't know what they're going through. Live your life and mind yours because no one deserves to be judged just like you don't want anybody to judge you.)

Grow Up

"When I was a child I played as a child, but when I became a man I put away childish things"

I wonder to myself sometimes, do you

I wonder when will you grow up boy or girl, man or woman

When are you going to stop with all of these childish things

ACT YOUR AGE NOT YOUR SHOESIZE

You are "grown" now and you are going to college still playing middle school games

You can't pull the same stunt, make the same jokes or pranks

What part don't you understand, the GROW or the UP

You don't appreciate this or life at all

Do you know how many people wish they had your place

Do you want to be that way for the rest of your life

I don't think so

Yes you are hearing it from the lips without the lipstick that left the life shit on your shoulder

Chicks and dudes

1+1=2 dumb plus dumb equals you

1+1=3 God the Holy Spirit and the Jesus in me

Stopping me from going crazy

Hitting you with reality

That you may not ever see at least not safely

Because safety isn't free

Only your stupidity

But you should let it free and maybe just maybe

It's a better you that people may want to see

The Letter L

I'm missing the L in my life
The letters behind it are there
The O-V-E but I just can't seem to find my L
Even the Y-O-U is there
Its hurts why doesn't it want to be found
Why can't I have my L
It made me smile, made me feel like a woman should
It completed me
Made me feel like I had my American dream
I loved it
And it loved me back
Instead of a gift card
It gave me homemade coupons
Sent me roses just because
And even edible arrangements
Took me on picnics and made up games to play
I enjoyed not spending money
And favored spending time
Massages at night because we both had a rough day
Peaceful movies at night
Soft music as we laid
My smile stretched as wide as the ocean
My heart as deep as the sea
But when it left me I burned inside
Down to my soul
I never knew of this feeling
It made me depressed as if my life was over and I'd never feel this way
again
I couldn't tell anybody or was tired of telling somebody

Tired of talking about it

Just wanted to be left alone

But was tired of being alone

I just wanted it back

I just wanted my L to make me feel whole again and like I could
accomplish anything

I feel empty and sad

I don't want anything else but to be thought of, cared for, and
appreciated

Something I could stay adjusted to

A casual thank you would do to

Just show me I'm not here for nothing

Let me know why I'm waiting for you

Tell me you'll be back

Why am I fighting for you, who are you and why me

How did I lose you

You made me assured that I was an original

Told me you knew I was it

Then I lost you

All I'm saying is I want my L-O-V-E Y-O-U back!

<u>Tired</u>

I'm tired

Sick and tired

I'm tired of being a woman

The things that come with being a woman is carrying the weight of the
world on your back

Everybody expects you to know you gone get your heart broke

But nobody told you how many times it would happen

There ain't no fury like a woman scorn because we take so much

Shit no man's anger could compare

A woman is suppose to cater to a man but when are we catered to

No matter how many hints we drop their remedial asses still don't know
what to do

I'm tired of compromising

And always having to smile when I'm dying inside

Tired of telling you wrong from right

Sick of not being held when I want to

Sick of always being the bigger person

When is it my turn to be babied

A woman has to do what she gotta do

But when is a man gone do what he's suppose to do

A woman has to go thru all the hard shit from heart break to babies

From teary eyes to lonely sighs

But we're suppose to get used to it

Why

Why do we always have to sacrifice our viginas', our hearts, our minds

We can't live with them

And can't live without them

So we put up with shit we don't deserve

A man will never understand how we feel

But can you tell me when will they try

They want us to be so beautiful and magnificent but

Make us feel like we ain't shit

Men don't want us to change but they get comfortable and change and

we can never get back the same man we once had

We stop getting I Love You's and the You're Beautiful's and the I Miss

You's

And we are expected to accept it

I'm tired

Sick and tired of being real

Being broken down and left for scrap pieces

<u>Used To</u>

I used to wonder
How could you praise somebody you don't see
I used to wonder
How could you love someone you don't know
But then I fought my thoughts from the devil
And kept my faith
I knew every time He allowed me to go through
He had a way for me to get out
When I felt like I had nothing to live for
He showed me why He created me
He gave me a purpose and I plan to fulfill it
I won't let no man of any kind bring me down!

Facebook.com

www.facebook.com
Compose message
Subject: balancing obscure ground and my concrete emotions
To him
FUCK YOU
My mom made it a constant reminder that it's better to be pissed of
than to be pissed on
So I'll subtract-vance so I can ad-vance in getting over you
I'm telling you, don't call, text, or even facebook me when you feel my
pain
I want to cut a piece of my agony and store it into your numb cabinet
heart so you can have what's rightfully yours
Once beautiful, now hideous
The correspondence we had
Like Leonardo's 13th chapel undone
Leaving me like a polar bear
Cold and lethargic
I want the thoughts of you to abandon my mind
Forsaken by his love, I bet
Blind like a nose
Your sweet aroma had me fooled
So I rest upon my queen size bed in my kush pillows n envision your
appalling, foul, grotesque horrid facial features
Overdoes on his lies and left my intuition behind
You emptied me like a garbage can on trash day
Took everything out of me and left me out in the open
Alone like oxygen in a secluded room
Seemingly being my best friend

I always have someone to talk to, to console me and wipe my tears away
Left me like a empty love seat
Drag mouse down and click send.

<u>Introduction of Part 2</u>

This is just an introduction of how I will put your addition in my part 2 edition of "Opinions of Young Mature Minds" as well as you letting me know what inspired you. Send what you want and it can possibly be in here as well.

Penny

Was it because of his rough texture or maybe his brown skin No one seems to notice him

I guess He never seems to make a difference unless your short a cent

Eighty nine of his friends a day could help a kid in an orphanage

Bodiless he only shows his head

People prefer paper instead from the comfort of his lint filled denim home from washer to dryer

Dryer to washer he practically did laundry on his on

Been around for so long he could have been a great grandfather

You see he was similar to the slaves passed from owner to owner, loaner to loaner,

Woman to man, hand to hand, and he was known for his great transaction skills Even though his freedom lied in the loss of others, the cost of others, he often suffer

Until one day he found his significant other

See she was a dime and they made a vowel to each other

If they were to ever die then they would meet up again in ocean's eleven

Cash register heaven and wait to be selected by some random consumer See I would have still been in heaven if it wasn't for the taxes on the tuna that she purchased

I blame Uncle Sam for my departure even though her taking me wasn't worth it You see we lined off in sections of fifty until the store owner lift me

Leaving forty nine of my kind behind to miss me

But I had family in all the cities and being raised in poverty

I learn to appreciate the little things if any

And to never under estimate the power of a penny

that grows to be a nickel, that grows to be a quarter that grows to be millions of dollars spent on a war worth not even fighting for but, yet we can't find a cure and my only fear is that we settle for less and think that we have plenty and under estimate the power of a

Penny

By: Willie Sowell

<u>A LOVE I WILL NEVER REGRET</u>

You're the love that I always prayed for,

Your smile is so precious and your lovely voice I just can't ignore,

The love that we share I could never ask for more,

Just to wake up and see your beautiful eyes is something that I truly adore,

The touch of your hands, and the taste of your kiss,

Not even in a million dreams could I imagine a love like this,

I've been truly blessed with an angel indeed,

To say I have the best is saying the least,

A true angel to me with everything I need,

To ask for more is words I could never breathe,

I saw something so special in you from the very first time we met,

So how can I ever say that you're a love that I regret.

By: Dymonique Burton

Hyphen

She was just a hyphen

Yearning to be an equal sign

In this world of periods and dollar signs

Where the battle for who gets the upper hand isn't so complex

Just check, who came first in this universe

Then, respect your elders

That flat line symbol never could accept that

This was how it was meant to be.

Every time she gave birth to a nation of "elders"

Something told her that, that philosophy was wrong.

That flattery shouldn't make her feel like the lithium in a dying car battery

That drama doesn't have to be identical to tragedy

So write her a script that ends like a fairy tale

Show her appreciation as clear as a glass slipper

Make her feel beautiful like the Big Dipper.

When you think of her . . .

Actually pin up stars,

Don't just look at pinup stars

And tuck away your evils in a box

And when it unlocks

Act like you never created it

By taking it and naming it Pandora.

Open up the doors on your mind.

Let a new way of thinking sink in.

Cause she,

And many others like her,

Are tired of feeling like rain,

During Spring Break,

On your birthday,

Dripping on your candles before a wish has a chance to be made.

Forced to fill in the role the bible carved out for her

By pulling Seneca Falls inwardly

And showing only trophy wife outwardly

Since that's the only way she can shine.

Praying that she drowns in the deep end

Since shallowness kills her every time.

She's tired of wondering that if ribs come in pairs . . .

Why is she the odd one out?!

Breathe life into the words printed from Kate Chopin's mouth.

Give her a new pair of billie's jeans

To mend her broken-mixtape spirit

Rip off the labels like

Sony . . . Panasonic . . .

Don't let her be another Stereo-type

Hanging by the strings of aprons,

Weighed down by dinner plates,

Obstructed by the friction of brooms . . .

Let her not be another Koolaid-smile in the room,

A cheap quarter-packet of goodness

Enjoyed only in the instant

That she holds your sugar-interest.

Be not afraid of showing signs of weakness

And uncripple your fingers from refusing to mint a female on a coin for more than four years.

Burn the image of her worth on your mind till it sears.

Tattoo a picture of nine months labor,

Lazor-print a pic of PMS behavior,

And it'll only make sense that Muhammad Ali had to have had an estrogen fist.

Be so kind as to love her blind.

So she knows you love her for who she is on the inside

And not for

Mary Kay

Maybelline

And L'Oreal on the outside

Cause all that makeup

Doesn't make up

For the fact that under the foundation

She's just a hyphen (-)

Hoping to one day be equal (=)

Like she was just a grammatical error

That change will come and correct,

Make her feel whole,

Notice her scars,

And whisper the words in her ear

That she'll hear only as . . .

Edit.

By: Thasia Madison

I Love Her

I love her

Yea I said it

I love her

And contrary to what you other motherfuckers may believe

I truly do love her

Hell it took me 2 years to show her that my heart has her lips impression

So this is her love poem selection

This feeling is so inebriating that can only be described as love

She is my vice my addiction

A high better than any drug

So what if I crack head fiend for her

She is my weakness

So her tear fall from my eyes

She is my strength

So her backbone is the I'm still standing

And I know I've fucked up in the past

But if I lost her I would cease to exist

Because she is my life force

She is my world my heart and my soul

She is my day light during my darkest nights

The sun sets and rises with her smile

The moon is buried deep within her eyes

So before I even knew her I had her tatted on my

She completes me

And at 78 I could still see us going strong

And yea I have others

But until 2 months ago those "haves" have become hads

And have more distance between me and em' then the past

I thought I knew what love was

But had it all wrong before I met her

Love at first sight wasn't quite it

But the love we made the first night

Felt like angels wings during flight

She makes me feel at peace

Like a moon and star at night

With 2 blunts a pen and a pad

She relieves me

She sets my soul on fire

She got my back more than spiral cards and vertebrates

And I never have to worry about being without the toasta

Because she is the 45 hosta

And she stay by my side and she ain't never scared to roast ya

That's right she be on some gutta shit

Crazier than any niggas gutta bitch

Call her a bitch and like crack ya brain will get flipped

Except for me

So I dedicate songs by Slim Thug cause that's my bitch

Fuck with my bitch and you will get yo ass kicked

I mean I love her more than my life

So harm her

And please believe I will end yours faster than Kimbo's last fight

She holds me down more than gravity

She'll be there till the end so I call her time

Tell her I'm cheating and she'll laugh

Cause' she knows that's a lie

She is the goddess that has me fighting temptation

And she so close to God that she could be my salvation

So this is her love dedication

And did I mention that I love her

By: Brittany Avie

If There Were No Black People

By Makebra Anderson

One morning, a little boy named Theo woke up and asked his mother, "Mom, what if there were no Black people in the world?"

His mother thought about that for a moment, and then said, "Son, follow me around today and lets just see what it would be like if there were no Black people in the world. Now go get dressed and we will get started."

Theo ran to his room to put on his clothes and shoes. His mother took one look at him and said, "Theo, where are your shoes? Son, I must iron your clothes. Why are they so wrinkled?

When she reached for the ironing board it was no longer there. You see, **Sarah Boone**, a Black woman, invented the ironing board and **Jan E. Matzelinger**, a Black man, invented the shoe lasting machine. The shoe lasting machine is a machine that attaches the top of the shoe to the sole.

"Oh well," she said, "Please go and do something to your hair." Theo ran in his room to comb his hair, but the comb was not there."

You see, **Walter Sammons**, a Black man, invented the comb.

Theo decided to just brush his hair, but the brush was gone. **Lydia O. Newman**, a Black female, invented the brush.

Well, this was a sight. Theo had no shoes, wrinkled clothes, and his hair was a mess. Even his mom's hair was a mess. See **Madam C. J. Walker** was one of the first African-American female entrepreneurs, and she created many hair care products for Black women.

Mom told Theo, "Let's do our chores around the house, and then take a trip to the grocery store."

Theo's job was to sweep the floor. He swept and swept and swept. When he reached for the dustpan, it was not there. You see, **Lloyd P. Ray**, a Black man, invented the dustpan.

So he swept his pile of dirt over in the corner and left it there. He then decided to mop the floor, but the mop was gone. You see, **Thomas W. Stewart**, a Black man, invented the mop.

Theo yelled to his Mom, "Mom, I'm not having any luck!"

"Well son," she said, "Let me finish washing these clothes and we will prepare a list for the grocery store."

When the wash finished, she went to place the clothes in the dryer, but it was not there. You see, **George T. Sampson**, a Black man, invented the clothes dryer.

Mom asked Theo to get a pencil and some paper to prepare their list for the market. So Theo ran for the paper and pencil but noticed that the pencil lead was broken. Well, he was out of luck because **John Love**, a Black man, invented the pencil sharpener.

Mom reached for a pen, but it was not there because **William Purvis**, a Black man, invented the fountain pen. As a matter of fact, **Lee Burridge** another Black man, invented the typewriting machine, and **W. A. Lovette**, another Black man, the advanced printing press.

Theo and his mother decided to head to the market. Well, when Theo opened the door he noticed the grass was almost 5 feet tall. You see, the lawn mower was invented by **John Burr**, a Black man.

They made their way over to the car and found that it just wouldn't go. You see, **Richard Spikes**, a Black man, invented the automatic gearshift and **Joseph Gammel** invented the supercharge system for internal combustion engines. Without these, the car wouldn't work. Gammel was also a Black man.

They noticed that the few cars that were moving were running into each other and having wrecks because there were no traffic signals. You see, **Garrett A. Morgan**, a Black man invented the traffic light.

Well, it was getting late, so they walked to the market, got their groceries and returned home. Just when they were about to put away the milk, eggs and butter, they noticed the refrigerator was gone. You see **John Standard**, a Black man, invented the refrigerator. So they just left the food on the counter.

By this time, Theo noticed he was getting mighty cold. Mom went to turn up the heat; however, **Alice Parker**, a Black female, invented the heating furnace so they didn't have heat. Even in the summer time they would have been out of luck because **Frederick Jones**, a Black man, invented the air conditioner.

It was almost time for Theo's father to arrive home. He usually took the bus. But there was no bus. Buses came from electric trolleys, which were invented by another Black man, **Elbert R. Robinson**. He usually took the elevator from his office on the 20th floor, but there was no elevator because **Alexander Miles**, a Black man, invented the elevator.

He also usually dropped off the office mail at a nearby mailbox, but it was no longer there because **Philip Downing**, a Black man, invented the letter drop mailbox and **William Barry**, another Black man, invented the postmarking and canceling machine which, which is how we get stamps.

Theo and his mother sat at the kitchen table with their head in their hands. When the father arrived he asked, "Why are you sitting in the dark?" Why? Because **Lewis Howard Latimer**, a Black man, invented the filament within the light bulb. Without a filament a light bulb won't turn on.

Theo quickly learned what it would be like if there were no Black people in the world. Daily life would be a lot more difficult, not to mention if he were ever sick and needed blood. **Charles Drew**, a Black scientist, found a way to preserve and store blood, which led to his starting the world's first blood bank.

And, what if a family member had to have heart surgery? This would not have been possible without **Dr. Daniel Hale Williams**, a Black doctor, who performed the first open heart surgery.

You don't have to wonder, like Theo, what the world would be like without African-Americans. It's clear, life as we know it would be very different!

Overview

Overall I hope you enjoyed my book. I talked about my opinions of the government, family issues, friends, love, sex, and anything that popped to my mind. As a teenager coming into adult hood, I feel you should be willing to learn about everything before you act so you will know the consequences of your own actions. I also feel that as an adult you should know that you are never too old to learn, you can learn from the young as well as we can learn from you. This book was basically just me expressing myself on what I think about sometimes and what I feel. I can't stress it enough about how you don't have to be super genius or a college this and that, to do something wonderful. It is goes from children's books, to how-to books, anybody can do it. Whether you agree or not I am proud of myself and glad of the accomplishment I've made especially at my age. Always remember (Sister Act 2), "If you wake up in the morning and all you can do is think about writing, then baby you a writer", and that goes for whatever you want to be. So again thanks for reading and appreciating my work. Opinions of my young mature mind, part 1.

Thanks

First off I give Thanks to my Lord and Savior Jesus Christ. Also I really just want to say thanks to everyone who believed in me and didn't tell me I couldn't do it or not to do it. For every person I felt I could tell about writing my book and not have to feel doubted or even ashamed, thank you. Thanks to my entire family, my real friends, those who helped and supported me, and those who bought my book. THANK YOU!!!!

About The Author

I decided to write this book at a young age as I kept thinking about things I wanted to do with my life and actually started at the age of 15. People may think, "She's too young, she doesn't know anything", but this book is original. I wanted to write about regular and normal everyday topics. Me, myself, personally, I like to read but if a book doesn't catch my attention I'll drop it. So I chose to do something different. I'm from Houston, Texas, born and raised and I grew up in a single parent home with my mom and my sister. I love my mom and everything she's done for me. She's sacrificed and worked and even went without things just so my sister and I can have whatever we needed. Unconditional love like that is very rare and someday I hope to be able to share that with my kids and hopefully husband too. My mom is in the army and after my first semester in middle school I went to move in with my aunt while my mom went to Alabama. So far that's where I was and I felt blessed that in 2008 my mom got to come back home. Altogether about me, it's simple; I'm a simple young lady from Houston, Texas, in the streets of 5th ward with big dreams and goals. I plan to make them all into realities and help others once I make it. I have a kind heart like my both of my grandma's and it makes me know that giving is way better than receiving. I believe that's what God made me for. My birthday is June 27, 1991 and that day was born a blessing to the world. I have always loved to sing, dance, write poetry, and do hair, anything with music /giving back, and speaking my mind. I have more dreams than just writing, this book is one, having my own organization, my own recreation centers and altogether my own empire. At the time of being a senior in high school I was Miss. Barbara Jordan 2008-2009, captain of the Kashmere Senior High School cheerleaders, a Mademoiselle Secretary and step master, Class of 2009 class officer, National Honor Society Member, proud A-B student, and more. I am now attending Prairie View A&M University with a major in business management and I plan to have a minor in music. This is where I am and the completion of my first book and hopefully you see me going further in the near future.

This book was a Part 1 because I believe a way for me to support my people is giving you all a chance to express yourselves. So if you want to add your own opinions or poetry and what inspired your art, please write me back at:

Brittany Phillips
P.O. Box 351
Prairie View, TX. 77446

The photos taken for this book were by Ryan Versey and you can contact him at: Bandgeek1@ymail.com